Wisdom of Buddhism

Introduction:

Buddhism is characterised by numerous wisdoms that stand for harmony and peaceful interaction with the environment. This is due to the teachings of the Buddha. He says that life is an endless cycle, which means that life has no beginning and no end. Man is determined by his actions in the present life for what he will be in the next life. Faith refers to life as suffering. Only those who act virtuously can escape this suffering and enter the so-called nirvana.

This book is about the most important wisdoms of Buddhism. These wisdoms serve both the believers of Buddhism and anyone else who has a need for harmony and peace. In particular, they are meant to help you find yourself, become more serene and be more mindful of your surroundings. Buddhist sayings are helpful in many life situations. Whether someone is angry, sad or afraid. In most life situations, it is enough to open this book and take a calming, comforting or strengthening piece of wisdom.

The wisdom in this book is divided into three chapters. Firstly, the wisdom of the "historical Buddha", the wisdom of the Zen faith and lastly the wisdom of the Dalai Lama who is still alive today.

Wisdoms according to Buddha (563 B.C. - 483 B.C.)

"Speak or act with a pure mind, and delight will follow you, like your shadow, unshakable."

"We are what we think. All that we are arises in our thoughts. With our thoughts we create the world."

"Never in the world does hate cease through hate. Hate ceases through love."

"If you want to know who you were, look at who you are. If you want to know who you will be, then look at what you are doing."

"If you want to know your future, look at yourself in the present, because it is the cause of your future."

"Do what you want, but not because you have to."

"Don't believe old manuscripts unconditionally, don't believe in anything at all just because people believe it - or because you have been made to believe it since childhood."

"Meditation means wisdom, lack of meditation means ignorance. Know what moves you forward and what inhibits you."

"Our appointment with life takes place in the present moment. And the meeting place is exactly where we are at the moment."

"Love for all beings is true religion."

"Every morning we are born again. What we do today matters most."

"It is no use just being a good person if you do nothing!"

"The best prayer is patience."

"Life is not a problem to be solved, but a reality to be experienced."

"A sweet word often refreshes more than water and shade."

"Thousands of candles can be lit by the light of one candle without its light dimming. Joy does not diminish when it is shared."

"To understand all is to forgive all."

"As the field is corrupted by weeds, so man is corrupted by his greed."

"The carpenter works the wood. The archer bends the bow. The wise man shapes himself."

"No one saves us but ourselves. No one can and no one must. We must walk the path ourselves."

"Speak with pure thoughts and happiness will follow you like your shadow."

"Be absorbed in your actions and think that it is your last act."

"Where everyone mingles noisily, you will never come to your senses."

"Each one of us is a god. Each one of us is omniscient. We have only to open our consciousness to listen to our own wisdom."

"The way is not in heaven. The way is in the heart."

"Mind is everything - what you think, you become."

"There is no path to happiness. Happiness is the way."

"Do not chain yourselves like slaves to beauty. But do not chain yourselves to suffering either. Everything is in flux, both pass away."

"The teaching is like a raft that you use to cross a river to the other shore, but you leave it behind and don't carry it around once it has served its purpose."

"Speak and act with an unclean spirit, and trouble will follow you."

"As the wheel follows the ox that draws the cart."

"Five rules remember for daily life: Always be compassionate and cherish the least life. Give and take freely, but never unseemly; never lie; be demure; avoid the poisons of pleasure; and always respect women."

"Holding on to anger is like drinking poison and expecting the other person to die as a result."

"The problem is that we think we have time."

"The noblest way to gain knowledge is through reflection and deliberation. The easiest way is through imitation and the bitterest way is through experience."

"In times when people become worse and true teaching perishes, the number of rules of law increases."

"Holding on to anger is like holding on to a red-hot piece of coal."

"Few realise that patience makes one patient."

"Past love is but a memory. Future love is a dream and a wish. Only in the present, in the here and now, can we truly love."

"Everything created is impermanent. Strive on, strive to be ceaselessly mindful."

"All human beings are one. What distinguishes them is the name you give them."

"If you have a problem, try to solve it. If you can't solve it, don't make it a problem."

"Carrying grudges is like grabbing a red-hot piece of coal with the intention of throwing it at someone. You only burn yourself in the process."

"Learn to let go, that is the key to happiness."
"Take time every day to sit still and listen to things. Pay attention to the melody of life that resonates within you."

"All our existence is fleeting like clouds in autumn; birth and death of beings appear like movement in dance. A life is like lightning in the sky; it rushes by like a torrent down a mountain."

"To travel well is better than to arrive."

"Where desire blossoms, suffering blooms. Where lust withers, sorrow withers."

"Two things you should avoid, O wanderer: purposeless desires and excessive mortification of the body."

"Do not dwell on the past, do not dream of the future. Concentrate on the present moment."

"Every day is a good day."

"What is the point of praying to gods? Is it not foolish to think that another can bring us bliss or misery?"

"Not outside, only within oneself should one seek peace. He who has found inner peace grasps at nothing, nor does he reject anything."

"Not the belief in a supreme being, nor its denial, but only one's own effort to live rightly and one's self-achieved spiritual development can lead to liberation."

"The secret of the extraordinary man is in most cases nothing but consequence."

"There is only one time when it is essential to wake up. That time is now."

"The way is not in heaven. The way is in the heart."

"What you think today, you will be tomorrow."

"Holding on to anger is like holding on to a red-hot piece of coal with the intention of throwing it at someone - the one who gets burnt is yourself."

"We are what we think. Everything we are arises from our thoughts. With our thoughts we shape the world."

"Poison does no harm to those whose hands are whole; evil does no harm to those who have not done it."

"Do not run after the past and do not lose yourself in the future. The past is no more. The future has not yet come. Life is here and now."

"Give up winning and find happiness."

"Those who wish to increase their wealth should take the bees as an example. They collect honey without destroying the flowers. They are even useful to the flowers. Gather your wealth without destroying its sources, and it will increase steadily."

"A man who learns little plods through life like an ox; in flesh he increases, but not in spirit."

"Every life has its measure of suffering. Sometimes this is what brings about our awakening."

"Calm as a deep lake in unclouded waters is the wise man with his serene clarity."

"Blessed is the man who is at peace with himself. There is no greater happiness on earth."

"There is a perfection deep in the midst of all inadequacy. There is a stillness deep in the midst of all perplexity. There is a purpose deep in the midst of all worldly cares and woes."

*"Believe nothing because a wise man has said it.
Believe nothing because everyone believes it.
Believe nothing because it is written.
Believe nothing because it is considered sacred.
Believe nothing because someone else believes it.
Believe only what you yourself have recognised as true."*

Wisdoms from Zen Buddhism

"You can only fill an empty bowl."

"The seeds of the past are the fruits of the future."

"If one tells a lie, a thousand others give it as truth."

"You cannot tread the path until you yourself have become the path."

"Do it or do not do it, but stop trying."

"Approach all things and all beings with the kindly face of mildness."

"If your gaze is even slightly clouded, you will see nothing but delusions."

"Be patient with each day of your life."
"Touch the emptiness in your life, and there flowers will bloom."

"Be present in everything you do. The only reality is now. As long as you are dwelling on the past or chasing the future, you are not really alive in the now."

"He who goes his own way grows wings."

"The awareness of not knowing is the beginning of the doubt that leads to wisdom."

"Smile at others - and you smile at your own heart, for they are like you."

"If a problem can be solved, why be unhappy? And if it cannot be solved, what is the point of being unhappy?"

"No snowflake falls on the wrong place."

"The sum of suffering in the world always remains constant."

"It is not because man is superior to other beings because he mercilessly martyres them, but because he is compassionate towards all living beings."

"If your mind is always completely empty, you will attain purity. But do not think of it, or you will lose it. If, however, you fall again into non-purity, simply pay no attention to it, and you will be free again."

"Knock on the sky and then listen to the sound."

"On the kind of thinking everything depends. From thinking everything emanates, everything is directed and created. Whoever speaks or acts badly, suffering follows him like the wheel follows the hooves of the draft animal."

"Whether one spends life laughing or crying, it is the same period of time,"

"To catch the butterfly of Zen in the net of the mind - let us realise that it cannot be done."

"The struggle in our consciousness, between right and wrong, leads to the disease of the mind."

"A blade of grass is a treasure and a treasure is a blade of grass."

"If you want to realise the truth, then don't be for something, but also don't be against something. The struggle between being for something or against something is the worst disease of human reason."

"If I let go of what is in me, it will set me free. If I hold on to what is within me, it will destroy me."

"The water that is too pure has no fish."

"When mindfulness touches on something beautiful, it reveals its beauty. When it touches on something painful, it transforms and heals it."

"Sitting still Doing nothing Spring comes The grass grows."

"The flower returns to the root."

"Life holds many detours. The art is to admire the landscape along the way."

"You smile - and the world changes."

"The teacher is there when the student is ready for it."

"For all beings, I want to unfold unlimited love, compassion, compassionate joy and equanimity, knowing that all living beings strive for happiness."

"Everything that blooms passes away."

"If you have an opinion about Buddhist teaching, it becomes a worldly thing. If you have no opinion about worldly things, they become Buddhist teaching."

"Free yourself from your self and act from your self."

"If you don't get it from yourself, where do you think you'll get it from?"

"Water solidifies into ice, ice melts into water. What is born dies again; what has died lives again. Water and ice are ultimately one. Life and death, both are well."

"Great understanding comes with great love."

"Now - This is it. - The whole purpose and meaning of all being."

"The rain has stopped, the clouds have cleared, the weather is clear again. When your heart is purified, all things in your world are purified. Let this fleeting world be, let yourself be. Then the moon and the flowers will accompany you on the great path."

"

Sun of Wisdom. O Victoress over Storm To study the Way is to study oneself. To study oneself is to forget oneself. To forget oneself is to become one with all existences."

Disciple: "I have nothing."
Master: "Then throw it away."

"When you do something, do it as well as you can. Don't pay attention to the result, the result is not important."

"The fearless hero is like a loving child."

"If you walk, then walk. When you stand, stand. And without wavering."

"If you want to go back to the source, then you must swim against the current."

"Choose a beautiful place in silence, sit down and be still. If you want to, then cry."

"When the mountain flowers bloom, their fragrance reveals the true meaning."

"O pure and shining radiance. O night-drifting flames. Thy glory fills the world."

"What is the greatest wisdom? Daily life."

"Misfortune is what happiness is based on. Happiness is what misfortune holds. Who knows the end?"

"When you understand that others are different from you, then you begin to become wise."
"See everything with your own eyes. If you hesitate, you will miss your life."

"Don't look for the truth, just stop having opinions about everything."

"Stop thinking about it and talking about it, and there is nothing you cannot know about it."

"Life is never just poverty."

"When you search? What is that but chasing sound and form? If thou seekest not? Then how are you different from earth, wood and stone? You must seek without seeking."

"The decisive thing is the doing, not so much the execution."
"Water heats slowly and boils suddenly."
"Seek out stillness and take the time and space to grow into your own dreams and goals."
"Throw your thoughts like autumn leaves into a blue river, watch them fall in and float away - and then: forget them."

"When the bow is broken and you have no arrows left, then shoot, shoot with your whole being."

"Before enlightenment: chop wood and carry water. After enlightenment: chop wood and carry water."

"A moment's patience, can prevent much harm."

"Before someone studies Zen, mountains are mountains and water is water; after a first glimpse into the truth of Zen, mountains are no longer mountains, and water is no longer water; after enlightenment, mountains are mountains again, and water is water again."

Wisdoms according to Dalai Lama (1935 - today)

"In anger, man loses his intelligence."

"Even the enemy is useful to us, because in order to feel compassion, we must practise tolerance, forgiveness and patience - and that makes anger evaporate."

"A prerequisite for peace is respect for otherness and for the diversity of life."

"Forgiveness or patience does not mean always accepting everything that others inflict on you."

"Our common Mother Nature is showing her children more and more clearly that she has run out of patience."

"Once a year, go to a place where you have never been before."

"Old friends die, new friends appear. It's like the days. An old day passes, a new one appears."

"Smile if you want a smile from another face."

"The foundation of world peace is compassion."

Spend some time with yourself every day.
"We live not to believe but to learn."

"Be kind whenever possible. It is always possible."

"Difficult times make us develop determination and inner strength."

"The world does not belong to the leaders. The world belongs to all humanity."

"Change is only brought about by active action, not by meditation or prayer alone."
"I will have kind thoughts towards others, I will not get angry or think badly of others. I will benefit others as much as I can."

"The planet doesn't need any more successful people. The planet desperately needs peacemakers, healers, innovators, storytellers and lovers of all kinds."

"If you lose, never lose the lesson!"

"In practising tolerance, the enemy is the best teacher."

"If you think you are too small to make a difference, try sleeping with a mosquito in the room."

"The best way to solve a problem in the human world is for all sides to sit down and talk."

"A clean environment is a human right."

"If a moral principle is missing, human life becomes worthless. Moral principle, truthfulness, is a key factor. If we lose that, then there is no future."

"Don't let the behaviour of others disturb your inner peace."

"Give those you love wings to fly away, reasons to come back and roots to stay."

"War is neither glamorous nor attractive. It is monstrous. It is inherently marked by tragedy and suffering."

"Our planet is our home, our only home. Where will we go if we destroy it?"

"The more you are motivated by love, the more fearless and free your actions will be."

"Sleep is the best meditation."

"Intelligence combined with compassion is the basis for global responsibility."

"There are only two days in a year when you can do nothing. One is yesterday, the other is tomorrow. This means that today is the right day to love, believe and first and foremost to live."

"Knowing and doing nothing is like not knowing."

"Irony has it that when we have attained the object of our desires, we are still not satisfied. In this way, desire never ends and is a constant source of trouble. The only antidote is frugality."

"He who begins everything with a smile will succeed in most things."

"Karma is an active process and has nothing to do with passive acceptance."

"Impatience and pride are among the main obstacles on the path." „Das Leben aller Lebewesen, seien sie nun Menschen, Tiere oder andere, ist kostbar, und alle haben dasselbe Recht, glücklich zu sein. Alles, was unseren Planeten bevölkert, die Vögel und die wilden Tiere sind unsere Gefährten. Sie sind Teil unserer Welt, wir teilen sie mit ihnen."

"Live a good, honourable life! When you're older and think back, you'll be able to enjoy it all over again."

"Man. He sacrifices his health to earn money. When he has it, he sacrifices it to get his health back. And he is so fixed on the future that he does not enjoy the present. The result is that he lives neither the present nor the future. He lives as if he will never die and eventually he dies without ever having lived properly."

"Respect yourself, respect others and take responsibility for what you do."

"Any cooperation is difficult as long as people are indifferent to the happiness of their fellow human beings."

"Remember that sometimes what you don't get can be a wonderful twist of fate."

"My faith helps me overcome negative feelings and find my balance."

"Open your arms to change, but don't lose sight of your values in the process."

"Compassion and love are not mere luxuries. As the source of inner and outer peace, they are fundamental to the survival of our species."

"The key to enjoying a happy and fulfilled life is the state of consciousness. That is the essence."

"Share your knowledge with others. This is a good way to achieve immortality."

Printed in Great Britain
by Amazon